cost of living

poems & nonfiction by

Brenna Womer

Finishing Line Press
Georgetown, Kentucky

cost of living

Copyright © 2022 by Brenna Womer
ISBN 978-1-64662-869-8 First Edition
All rights reserved under International and Pan-American Copyright Conventions. No part of this book may be reproduced in any manner whatsoever without written permission from the publisher, except in the case of brief quotations embodied in critical articles and reviews.

ACKNOWLEDGMENTS

Thanks to the following journals for publishing some of the works contained in this chapbook:

"Rot" in *Oyez Review*
"cost of living" in *North American Review*
"a liberation" in *Birdcoat Quarterly*
"a room, unfinished" in *Bellingham Review*
"Cape Fair" in *Cimarron Review*
"piecemeal" in *Juked*
"Go" in *Sixth Finch*
"It's the end of the world as we know it" in *Cleaver Magazine*
"Distancing" in *Bending Genres*
"When the job you worked your ass off for is given to an older white man with a soul patch, you ask your husband to fuck you with the lights on" in *Free State Review*

Publisher: Leah Huete de Maines
Editor: Christen Kincaid
Cover Art: Audrey Bertoia
Author Photo: Riley Fields
Cover Design: Elizabeth Maines McCleavy

Order online: www.finishinglinepress.com
also available on amazon.com

Author inquiries and mail orders:
Finishing Line Press
PO Box 1626
Georgetown, Kentucky 40324
USA

Table of Contents

Rot 1

cost of living 4

a liberation 5

a room, unfinished 7

Cape Fair 9

piecemeal 13

Go 14

It's the end of the world as we know it 15

Distancing 16

When the job you worked your ass off for is given to an older white man with a soul patch, you ask your husband to fuck you with the lights on 18

for Evan and Basil

Rot

My bottom molars are concave and pitted like the surface of the moon; they ache when I chew. I've been grinding my teeth since I was a child, and there's one tooth worse off than the rest, on my right side, with a crater the size of a raspberry seed. When one gets stuck from fresh fruit or jam, I can feel it, the small bit of resistance. Each seed beds down so deep that I almost feel bad excavating such a perfect fit with the nub of a bobby pin, tweezers or a pencil tip.

When I was a kid, a dentist told my mother I'd grow out of the grinding, but when I hadn't in a few years, she brought it up to a different dentist who suggested a nightguard we couldn't afford. Instead, my mother bought one of those boil-and-bite mouthguards for athletes; it was blue plastic and felt like hot tar against my gums when I bit for the impression. My mother held it out with a pair of tongs, and I wondered whether I should be putting something in my mouth that was too hot for her to hold.

When we eventually found a dentist who made nightguards for cheap, the fit was off, so I spit it out in my sleep. In the morning, I'd pick it up off the floor, stuck with dog hair and carpet fibers. I stopped wearing it, and my mother stopped asking.

*

I don't go to the dentist as often as I should. I got sick of the gasps and tuts and same-old questions when I open to reveal cheeksful of ravaged enamel. Instead, for the past decade, I've been budgeting for Sensodyne and chewing food on the left side of my mouth, which, for some reason, is achieving a slower rate of deterioration. In the last year, though, I got my first job with benefits, and it seemed foolish not to take advantage of my plan after seeing how much I pay for it.

The hygienist asked questions I couldn't answer with her hands in my mouth, but before she tilted me back, I asked her not to gasp, and she didn't. When the dentist came, he said I needed a cap on my raspberry molar and then asked if I'm bulimic without ever actually saying the word.

"We rarely see this level of wear without there being *contributing factors.*"

I said my experiences with bulimia were sporadic and long past, and he seemed satisfied:

"I trust you'd tell me," he said, "if that were the case."

At my follow-up appointment, the receptionist ran my card for an amount just shy of that month's paycheck, and when it didn't decline, I was ushered to a chair with a soft blanket and a nitrous mask. During the procedure, the hygienist smeared balm on my lips when they went dry, and under the influence, I was sure I'd never been touched with such tenderness by another person; I thought the dentist, with his drill, might be etching his own miniature Mount Rushmore into what was left of my unfortunate tooth, a secret colonization.

They 3D-printed my new molar, or else a machine carved it from a ceramic cube. Either way, the hygienist held it up for me to see, and said it was what my tooth was always meant to look like. It was underwhelming, all convex and beefy, without any pits for seeds.

*

When it was fitted and sealed, the dentist told me it could be sensitive for up to a week and to be patient, but it's been two months, and I still can't chew on the right side of my mouth. Last week, on my way home from work, I tilted the rearview mirror down at a stoplight and dropped my jaw for a look. In the daylight, I could see a shock of black emerging beneath the opaque surface, like ink a glass of 2%.

Every day, the black gets blacker, the tooth still aches, and I'm still short a paycheck because I agreed to the handwritten deductible scrawled on a sheet of letterhead. And I know I need to call the receptionist, to tell her about the black and the ache so I can open up my mouth again for the people, so they can get it right this time. But every day, I drive past the storefront and keep on driving. Every day, I don't make the call.

cost of living

i came home to a
tax collector; he
wanted to break
my bones, to age me
like a stone, to be
my mother.

i offered him a glass
of milk, and he drank
two; the dog and i
could smell his feet
through his shoes. he
asked for a list:

anything, he said, *that
might fetch a price*, but
you've eaten the last of
your mother's apple pie,
and there's no place, yet,
to sell a memory.

i brought him your
robe, all-gray like fur
and the dog's favorite;
the teaspoon i know
is a teaspoon but doesn't
say so, doesn't have to.

he said, *it's not enough,*
but i told him it has to be.

a liberation

i.
a lime that is ripe
and left unpicked belongs to
the one who picks it

    and when nobody picks the limes
    from the alley tree of the ruined
    house on tulip, i take them for myself;
    ripeheavy, dim citrus breaks
    the back of its elastic grace;
    it begs

ii.
a palmetto bug
is a cockroach when it is
crawling in your bed

    soft-white light through a window
    at the rear, exposed bulb and pull string
    above café curtains; either one person
    or twelve live inside, and maybe once
    a baby; pink highchair dirty plastic fisher
    price on the porch, i make a bowl of my shirt
    the first time, yes, the *first* time

iii.
do not forget to
draw a map back to your source
of rampant yielding

    across the street still on tulip
    a splinter of a house with a sign out front
    and no tenants just cicadas on the mailbox;

everything overgrown, but the tree
out front is fucking studded; it's hung
as shit with pale pith, and maybe this
is how it feels to be rich: too much to pick
or, at least, too much to carry.

a room, unfinished

does it end, forgotten darling—
the earth
your rope
what it feels like to know?

everything is a door,
an escape from the light; I
woke up to name the darkness
       the lavender, parting
            lakes traced open;
remind my heart of the ground,
that the world turns for the devil just the same.

can we know what is holy,
      early boy?
            painter, daydreamer
fire from the womb
    of a child bride,
a mother wed to this earth, to
the dirt, and pronounced
         forever young
by the prince of darkness or
dead leaves

I've lost patience with remembering, and
trust nothing but your open mouth

are we so bitter and blown-out to ask—
               is this all there is?
fuck me into silence on the eve
     we lose our shadows,
and light my bones like a candle
so I don't break you in the dark.

are we alone,
        forgotten darling,
                waiting on some blue wound,
looking for the other half of a woman,
sun-hungry   lost   and losing sight?

it's late,
your face is sand,
and we are running out of night.

Cape Fair

There is a house on an acre of land in Southwest Missouri that was built by three Amish men and their sons. My grandfather is dying there, now—has decided to die by concentration of ammonia in his blood, of liver disease.

His brothers have traveled with their wives from Texas and Florida, his eldest daughter from Arkansas, and his youngest, a son, from Southern California. My mother is the middle child, always her father's favorite—bookish and quiet. She's the child he never had to worry about, the one who lives nearby and knows to make the coffee so weak you can see to the bottom of a full mug, just how he likes it.

When I was a child, I loved my grandfather with an awkward desperation; I'd do anything for his attention but could sense I wore on his nerves. Sometimes during our visits, he'd let me sit in his den and watch low-budget horror and sci-fi movies while he worked on his stamp collection, but I asked too many questions and touched things I wasn't supposed to, left fingerprints on the glass of his Navy shadowboxes and replica submarines. He did love me then, though, when I attended Sunday school and helped my grandmother brown hamburger for tostadas, when I begged to read the poetry he wrote and kept in his desk drawer, with their ABAB rhyme schemes riddled with misspellings. The family has always been so proud of his poetry.

I don't know when he stopped loving me, only the moment I understood he didn't anymore, or that some sort of bad outweighed whatever good he still felt toward me. I was 16, and my mother and I were living with her parents for the summer while my father was on his last deployment to the Middle East. She and I attended the First Baptist Church of Cape Fair where my grandfather served as a deacon, or still does. Though, I assume it's more of an honorary title now that he can't walk stairs or count his own dice during Yahtzee.

It was during youth group in the basement while the adults were upstairs for Wednesday-night service—my grandmother in the nursery, my grandfather ushering the collection plate, my mother sitting alone in a pew. I was talking to the pastor's son, the only other high schooler I knew, trying to impress him with parroted information about local fishing prospects:

"My grandpa's the one who taught me how to clean a fish. Last week, I asked if he'd take me fishing on Table Rock, but he says the Lake is way too high right now, so I guess we have to wait."

The pastor's son looked confused, shook his head, and said, "Yeah, that's not really the way it works. Fishing's better when the Lake is up. And anyway, your grandpa went fishing with my dad a couple days ago. Not sure why he told you that."

My grandfather took me fishing for the first time when I was eight. Mom, Dad, and I had driven from Altus Air Force Base, Oklahoma, to the San Diego suburb where my grandparents lived for 25 years before settling in rural Missouri. Their two-bedroom in Santee barely fit the dozen of us who showed for the holidays every other year. There was a front-porch swing and a white couch I wasn't allowed to sit on except for Christmas morning. The centerpiece of the back patio was an enormous shell chandelier my mom brought back from the Philippines where she was stationed in her early 20s before she met my dad, and the entire house, especially the towels, smelled like my grandmother's perfume.

I always knew love in that house, but I was easier to love then. I was compliant when I was a kid, too afraid of testing the waters. I do wonder, though, when my grandfather realized I wouldn't always be so easy, that one day his age and our shared DNA wouldn't be enough to warrant my respect or admiration without effort. Only sometimes do I wish I had tried harder to keep being the granddaughter he could love—a woman of god, servant of men, bearer of children, and holder of my tongue; a woman who gives her respect before asking it in return.

My mother called me one night a few months ago to check in, but mostly, I think, to tell me that her father, a Type 2 diabetic, was in the hospital after he snuck a bag of marshmallows from the pantry while nobody was watching and ate them, one by one, until the plastic was empty. This was before he quit his treatments and medications, before everyone understood that he's dying on purpose.

The doctors have been cautioning his weight for a decade, but he's too angry and stubborn for a diet; my grandmother has tried. I always knew him with a bit of a belly. He's Italian, and my grandmother is Hispanic, so we ate big meals—pans of lasagna and platters of Mexican rice—but when they lived on the West Coast, he went out several nights a week to metal detect the beaches. I remember his calves so strong they looked like skin stretched over softballs from hours walking through sand. These days, though, he's so heavy he has trouble getting from room to room, his head like a rounded scoop of ice cream melting into his shirt collar.

When I was a teenager, my mother told me how she and her father would stay up later than the rest of the family, would drink coffee together in the middle of the night at the kitchenette. She said he wasn't always so conservative, that he admitted to her during those late-night talks that he wasn't sold on absolutes or capital-T truths, and I think she held on to that version of her father in the decades that followed.

My mother is a woman who is all-in until she's out, devout until she's apostate, in every regard except her family. She seems a bottomless well of compassion and understanding in the face of being silenced, criticized, ignored, and taken advantage of by those she loves. There has to be a word for it: the rage and indignation felt on behalf of a person who does not feel it for themselves. As a woman in her 50s, my mother is coming into her own. She's converted to Catholicism and is planning a pilgrimage through Northern Spain. She's also watching her father die in real-time, having her last coherent moments with him. I think she expected wisdom and perspective, moments from their 1980s kitchenette before she loses him for good. Instead, she's found herself risking vulnerability with the dogmatic grandfather I grew up with rather than the uncertain father she did, a man who was fucked up and absent and sometimes cruel but who was real when she needed him to be.

I'm not sad my grandfather is dying, and I won't make the trip to Cape Fair to say goodbye. We never did have much to say to each other, and anymore I have as little interest in reading his poetry as he has in reading mine. I've heard it's lucky, the easy way I have of cutting ties and moving on with life, of letting go. But sometimes it makes me feel broken, like I'm missing something inherently human that I don't think of blood the way others seem to or feel beholden to people for existing so I could exist too.

There's a line from Toni Morrison's *Beloved*, when Sethe says, "Love is or it ain't. Thin love ain't love at all," and every time I read it, I know it bone deep. I have no interest in a love that is not specific to me, that is not rich and full and without condition; I have no interest in love out of obligation or familiarity, because it's too easy. Blood is too easy a reason for love.

piecemeal

a rose by any other name would dissolve
in a jar of acid, could transition from one
state to another to no state ever again, to
nothing but something that was
just moments ago;

I was born breech, a blemish,
with my moon in the cancer
of a hospital bedsheet, in the early-
morning light of a slipping sun—

I was afraid of you; I'll say it
now:

I was afraid
         of you—

the bitter pill, swallowed, or was it
sweet, because the meat of me is
raw and wet and everything hurts
except coffee with cream, or whiskey
neat, and a Sausage McMuffin, a pill
so small it seems impossible strength
to stop the making, the feast.

Go

Loving you was finding the stall // in the food-court bathroom of the Battlefield // Mall with a toilet that wasn't already shit-stained // or floating a bloated tampon in a bowl of red wet //

two pale drops of piss I absorbed // off the peeling seat with a wad of single ply before // putting down a seat cover I never learned // to employ without compromising integrity //

You were an act of desperation // of holding the stall door closed with my foot // and trying not to breathe in // the overflow from the metal trashcan // loving you, if it had to be done, was fine

for a moment in time // it was fine

It's the end of the world as we know it

While shopping what's left of the canned goods at the grocery store, an announcement at the top of the hour, robust and autotuned: "All employees must now perform a personal temperature check," and I, in a pair of disposable vinyl gloves but not a facemask because Dr. Gupta says they're unnecessary for the still- and now- and currently-healthy, holding the last can of Kroger no-salt garbanzos, recall they've always made this announcement, but two weeks ago they were checking the temperature of the meats.

Distancing

My husband lost his job at the airport, in this Colorado mountain town of 6,500, because the last flight he worked for United had a single passenger. All the stores and restaurants are closed, all nonessential businesses, so he applied for a job at the hospital as a sanitizer; *They're desperate*, he said. Today, he was fitted for an N95 respirator mask, had three blood-draws, was pricked for TB; though, if the Senate bill passes, he'd likely make more on unemployment, *But that's not the point*, he says. *I want to look back on this time and know I helped people, that I was useful.*

I can see him from our living-room window, across the street at the food pantry where he volunteers on Wednesdays, bringing out prepackaged boxes for patrons, no one allowed inside the building now except for volunteers—Javier, Dusto, my husband, and a high schooler named Maria. Wednesdays are dedicated to the area's Spanish speakers, and he's been diligent about his Duolingo lessons. Every night I hear him in his office, *Sí, me gusta la ensalada de frutas,* followed by the trill that confirms a correct response.

At home, the tattoos on my hands are ashy and cracked because I wash them when I need to and when I don't. He brought me a mask, too, from the hospital, the disposable kind with the ear-loops. *You can wear it to the grocery store*, he says, sweetly, because he knows I'm already wearing vinyl gloves while I shop. Six years ago, I was diagnosed with hypochondria, and I'm still medicated for it, and other things, now. He always invites me to go with him to the pantry, and I'd planned to before the virus drove us all indoors. But he still goes, despite the risks, because he knows the odds are in our favor as late-20- and early-30-somethings. I know the statistics, too—we watch the news together—but they don't comfort me the way they do him, which I also know is part of my illness, the intimate understanding that I'm just as likely to be one of the unlucky few as the next 20-something. Maybe it's narcissistic, thinking I could always be the worst-case scenario, the exception rather than the rule.

I grew up delivering for Meals on Wheels with my mother, sitting in the back seat with stacks of Styrofoam clamshells that smelled like wet turkey stuffing and boiled brussels sprouts. When we were stationed in Altus, Oklahoma, we had a regular route and, on it, Mom's favorite delivery to a chatty old man named Clarence who lived in a trailer next to a tree on a dirt patch out in the country. I stayed in the car with the meals and watched from the window as she approached the doors of homes.

I was a nervous child, always, undiagnosed for what is clear to both of us now—OCD, general anxiety, the seeds of depression like she's struggled with, too, since childhood. I don't know what I expected to happen when people opened their doors to her, reaching for the slippery, lukewarm containers, but I always expected it. Occasionally, they'd ask her to come inside and carry the meals to the kitchen, and when my mother disappeared through the doorway, I held my breath until I could see her again. She'd walk back to the car, lock the doors with us inside, and head for the next stop, but I wished we could stay in the in-between, just the two of us, together, alone.

I understand my husband's impulse to help rather than to take, to use the privilege of our age and uncompromised immune systems for the good of others. I understand it because I grew up with it, and part of my mother's heart lives in me, beating right alongside my own; my husband learned it from his mother, too. But most of me wants to beg him, every day, not to leave, to lock our door to the world until it's safe again to stand within six feet of another human; to keep washing my hands and watch the seasons change from the windows while the government pays our rent. Most of me wants to exist as an island with the person I love, healthy in our little bubble, listening only to the one heart and not the imploring second, just the two of us, together, alone.

when the job you worked your ass off for is given to an older white man with a soul patch, you ask your husband to fuck you with the lights on

and he obliges, because he loves you and also loves fucking you // he's good at it, but even still, you have to try not to think about campus visits and job talks // about the novel you haven't worked on in months // about the ten pounds you've gained (at least) since taking this job in the first place, since moving to a valley in Colorado, between mountain ranges you don't love the way everyone else does, mountains that only ever looked like piles of cash, too rich for your blood, thicker at 7,000 feet // about the young men in your lit class who say Harjo is whiny and Bechdel is boring and that Octavia Butler really was writing about slavery when she says she wasn't writing about slavery, who tell you they wouldn't have taken your class if they'd known how depressing it would be, learning what it means to live as a woman in their world // but they'll like the new guy, or else won't give him much trouble, because he looks like what a professor should look like—lanky, glasses, balding, shirt & tie // and you guess he's probably never had a student flirt with him in a free-write or try to talk to him about girl problems during office hours // probably not // and you know you won't come with your husband fucking you like this, and he knows it too, but he also knows you're hurt and angry and that this is the first time you're not crying in days, so you know he won't stop fucking you until you tell him to; grab the vibrator off the nightstand and close your eyes.

Brenna Womer is an experimental prose writer and poet in flux. She is the author of *honeypot* (Spuyten Duyvil, 2019), *Unbrained* (FlowerSong Press, 2023), and two chapbooks. Her work has appeared in *North American Review, Crazyhorse, Indiana Review, DIAGRAM, The Pinch,* and elsewhere. She is a Visiting Assistant Professor of Creative Writing at Washington and Lee University and the interim editor of *Shenandoah*.

www.ingramcontent.com/pod-product-compliance
Lightning Source LLC
LaVergne TN
LVHW041526070426
835507LV00013B/1841